The Greater Serengeti from A to Z

A Safari in Pictures and Poetry

Stanley Fraley

To Ellen and Tony,

Stan Fraley

6/28/2016

DEAR ELLEN AND TONY,
WITH LOVE
NOW AND ALWAYS ♡

Huei (THE PHOTOGRAPHER ☺)

ACKNOWLEDGMENTS

The pictures were taken on a safari organized by Africa Dream Safaris. The animals were photographed by either Huri Fraley or Stanley Fraley during that safari.

Aardwolf

The aardwolf is a nocturnal animal. It rests in underground burrows during the day and emerges at night to seek food. It has a long, sticky tongue which it uses almost exclusively to eat termites. An aardwolf can eat several hundred thousand termites every night. It does not dig into termite piles but uses its tongue to lick them off the ground when the termites come out at night.

Aardwolves have a mane on their back that stands up when they feel stress. The aardwolf in the picture to the right clearly was not happy that we were getting close enough to it to take its picture.

A is for Aardwolf

An aardwolf in the wild is quite a rare sight.
It is scarce and it prowls mainly at night.
Though its Mohawk is raised while under fright,
Only termites should fear the threat of its bite

Cape Buffalo

Cape buffaloes are a subspecies of the African Buffalo. They are found in the Serengeti. They are bovines. Other bovines include cattle and oxen.

Terms used to describe individual Cape buffaloes include bulls, calves, and females. (If you want to have fun in a confusing sort of way try to understand that "cattle" is a collective word that is plural for which no true singular form exists. "Cow" is often used as the singular form for cattle, but in a strict sense a cow is a female from the cattle collective that has given birth to a calf. Before it has given birth it is a heifer. This is, of course, as opposed to adult males that are bulls or steers.)

Not sure who is braver above, the bird taking insects off the buffalo or the buffalo letting the bird that close to his eye. The bird seems to be the safest!

B is for Buffalo

Cape buffaloes don't look poetic
Though to some this might seem too brash.
But his comb over is just pathetic
Or perhaps it's a high brow mustache.

Cheetah

Cheetahs are the fastest land animal. They can run at speeds up to 70 mph, but for less than a minute. It only takes about 3 seconds to reach these speeds. The length of time it can maintain these high speeds is limited by overheating. After a sprint it needs to rest for up to 30 minutes to cool back down.

Lions roar, but cheetahs purr.

We were able to observe a "flirting" pair of cheetahs from a distance of about 30 feet and were able to hear them purring while taking the picture above! In the picture to the right she is not turning her back on him because of something he said. They are just scanning the horizon to make sure there are no threats they should worry about before returning to lounging together.

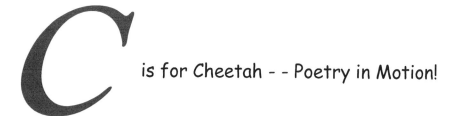

C is for Cheetah - - Poetry in Motion!

The cheetah can run the fastest they say,
It streaks with a shape sleek and narrow,
Using quick pulsing strides it chases its prey
With its head moving straight as an arrow.

Dik-dik

A dik-dik is a dwarf antelope. They are monogamous and usually mate for life. There are several different species of dik-dik. Kirk's dik-dik is the largest. The picture to the right is of a male Kirk's dik-dik. The males are slightly smaller than the females. Dik-diks are named for the alarm calls of the females. The males have small horns, which are about 3 or 4 in (10 cm) long. The horns are grooved and slanted backwards.

The bare black spot below the inside corner of each eye contains a scent gland that produces a dark, sticky secretion used to mark their territories. Both males and females have these scent glands. Their diet mainly consists of foliage, buds, and shoots, with little or no grass.

Dik-diks establish a series of runways through and around the borders of their territories that they can use when they are threatened.

 is for Dik-dik

A dik-dik is an antelope fair

That mates for life with a strong bond quite rare.

If something should happen to one of the pair,

The other soon dies overwhelmed by despair.

Eland

The "common eland" found in the Serengeti is the second largest antelope in the world. (It is just slightly smaller than the giant eland, which is called "giant" because of its large horns. Only the common eland are found in the Serengeti.) A male adult eland is about five feet high (shoulder) and can weigh up to about 2000 lbs, with an average weight closer to 1300 lbs. (This average size is comparable to large riding horses.)

About 12,000 to 18,000 eland participate in the Serengeti migration, along with the more numerous wildebeest, zebras and Thomson's gazelles. They are somewhat difficult to photograph because they avoid vehicles.

E is for Eland

The stately eland is a shy antelope.

It is big and compared to a horse.

But it survives quite well with no need to mope.

For its shyness it has no remorse.

Bat-eared Fox

The bat-eared fox uses its large ears to locate prey, which are predominately termites. The jaws are designed so that they are able to open and close 5 times per second.

F is for Bat-eared Fox

The bat-eared fox is known most for its ears.
They are large and help locate its food.
But for termites its jaws are the source of their fears
And its five bites per second they just think rude.

Masai Giraffe

Masai giraffes are the tallest land animal. The males grow up to about 19 feet tall. They are vegetarians and are uniquely capable of eating the leaves on Acacia trees. In addition to being tall enough to reach the leaves, their tongues and lips allow them to reach around the thorns.

The Masai Giraffe also have strong legs and sharp hooves. Most predators won't attempt to attack an adult since they can be killed with one swift kick.

 is for Giraffe

The giraffe is a strict herbivore
Where carnivores oft wear the crown.
But they still normally yield him the floor.
Next to him none can look down.

Rock Hyrax

Hyrax are the closest land animal relative of elephants. They also have rudimentary tusks that are used for defense and grooming. These tusks force the hyrax to use the molars on the sides of their mouths for food collecting and chewing. Rock hyrax are social animals and have a number of unique sounds which they link in a variety of songs. Google Rock Hyrax songs!

H is for Rock Hyrax

Rock hyrax are elephants' distant in-laws
With small tusks for defense, when not gabbing.
Thus they eat using teeth on the sides of their jaws,
Since they lack a proboscis for grabbing.

Impala

Boys' Club

Most mature male impalas live in a boys' club for at least some periods during their life.

Female Group

Physically strong, mature "Lucky" males establish their own territories and try to control female groups that wander in, as well as to defend it from other males.

Lucky males with their noses in the air are sampling the scents left by the females to see if one is ready to mate. This must be done often since such opportunities are fleeting. After a few months of expending energy to try to control the females and with very little time to graze, the male may lose the physical strength needed to maintain its territory and will end up back in the boys' club for some time to regain its strength.

I is for Impala

Territorial male (Lucky Boy) performing urine test on mate candidates that wandered into his territory.

Lucky male impalas spend months of their lives

Working to keep and control many wives.

When his strength does fail

The old boys he will hail

And join them while hoping his health soon revives.

Jackal

Jackals have a reputation of being cunning, sly animals. They also often appear in folklore tales using their intelligence and cunning to outsmart their enemies.

Thus "The Day of the Jackal," by Frederick Forsyth, 1973, was a novel, turned into subsequent movies, about a cunning, sly assassin hired to assassinate French President Charles de Gaulle. The assassin was known as the Jackal. In the novel the assassin fails. Thus real jackals are not sure the protagonist in that novel deserves his title!

J is for Jackal

Jackals are sly but to some they are prey.
Thus they dream of a Fred Forsyth novel,
Where their Jackal wins 'most every day
And assassins make hyenas grovel.

Lion

The lion is clearly the top predator in the Serengeti. Since lions hunt mainly at night they can be seen in various sleeping/resting poses in daytime. It is clear from their "relaxed" attitude while they are resting that they are not concerned about being attacked by other predators.

 is for Lion - - The King of the Serengeti

Noble Pose

Typical Pose

That the lion is King is a valid belief.

And his pose is oft noble when seen in relief.

Though when seen from an eagle,

They don't always look regal,

It's because no one else gives them grief.

Leopard

Leopards normally hunt at night. If seen during daytime they are usually spotted resting in a tree.

The leopard in the picture to the right had just made a kill. With some difficulty it had just dragged the antelope into a secluded location in some bushes. Leopards prefer to take their kill up into a tree so that they are better able to protect it from other predators such as lions or hyenas. Although they are capable of taking a carcass weighing as much as their own body weight into a tree, there were no suitable trees very close by and the leopard seemed to want to consume part of the kill before it tried to move it to a tree and up out of the reach of others.

L is for Leopard

A leopard kill in the day is a rare sight,

Since a leopard hunts game mainly at night.

A day stroll without fear

May be the last for those near,

'cause it kills by its bite and not fright.

Marabou Stork

The above Marabou stork is hanging out next to a trash can hoping that someone will bring some leftovers before he gets called to make a delivery himself.

M

 is for Marabou Stork

A Marabou stork has a huge wing span,

Which it needs for delivering babies.

Since its favorite dive is a full trash can,

We're just glad that they don't come with rabies.

Nile Crocodile

The Nile crocodile is the second largest reptile, smaller only to the seawater crocodile. It is an effective predator that uses ambush as its technique for catching prey. It has a very strong bite, but very weak muscles for opening its jaw.

The story for the pictures above and to the right is "two photographers, two cameras, one crocodile."

N

is for Nile Crocodile

A Nile crocodile can live a long while
Though it's far from the real Nile River.
Hiding under the water is the croc's hunting style,
While it awaits what the river will deliver.

Ostrich

An ostrich is the largest bird. It also has the largest eye of any land animal. Its kick is powerful enough to provide an effective weapon. Ostriches appear to wander the Serengeti largely without fear.

O

is for Ostrich

An ostrich is a bird, I've heard,

With whom I won't mess, I confess.

As a bird without flight, it still can fight.

It's quite big and not small, at all.

In a race it'd be fast, and not the last.

If I were nine feet tall we could look eye to eye,

But I'm not tall or fast so I'll just wave good-bye.

Elephant

In 1973 a local radio station had a pachyderm poetry contest. The poem to the right was my winning entry. But my favorite submission was:

> If an elephant parade you happen to see
>
> To these rules you ought to be hep,
>
> Up front or astride is where all wish to be,
>
> For behind you must watch your step.

P is for Elephant...in Pachyderm Poetry

An elephant is the largest land animal
With a heart that is strong and the purist.
And he's friendly, they say, to all large or small.
Still I pity his poor manicurist.

Female Cheetah

Pregnant cheetah

Q is for Female Cheetah—Queen of the Serengeti

A cheetah is a thing of beauty,
Who with cubs always knows her duty.
Though her duties she knows,
There are times she still shows
That at will she can be quite a cutie.

Rhinoceros

The so-called "White Rhino" is a rhino with a wide mouth. It is widely assumed that this is a result derived from white being confused with the Dutch wijde, meaning wide. The other species of rhino, with the smaller pointed mouth, then became the Black Rhino, even though both are grey. It is the case, however, that the color seen is largely determined by the color of the mud they roll in, and whether or not it is dried up. Both rhinos in the picture to the right are Black Rhinos.

Ogden Nash wrote a poem that starts out: The rhino is a homely beast, for human eyes he's not a feast... He has also written a number of other humorous poems about animals.

R is for Rhino

White is white and black is black
If you don't slur your words like some winos.
Because "wide" became "white", 'tis known as a fact,
Because of the mouths of "White" Rhinos.

Serval Cat

For its size, servals have the longest legs of the "big cats." It uses them to jump up and catch or swat down birds in flight. It will also pounce on any small animals in its vicinity, that it locates mainly by its sensitive hearing.

 is for Serval Cat

The serval's legs are the longest per ounce.

It can catch birds in flight with a ten foot high bounce.

With long ears that rotate

Using faint sounds to locate

It can spring out twelve feet to kill prey with a pounce.

Topi

Topi are easily distinguished from other antelopes because of their unique coloring.

T is for Topi

High fashion the Topi seem to show
When appearing upon the scenes.
Still the thing that I wish most to know
Is the brand of their cool blue jeans.

Warthog

Female warthogs are said to have four teats, and not more than four piglets. Each piglet will suckle from its chosen teat exclusively, even if another should become available. Perhaps it is because each little piglet (who knows it is pretty) sees its siblings and figures that they must be suckling from the wrong place since they turned out ugly!

U is for Warthog (An Even-toed Ungulate, not just because it's Ugly!)

Young warthogs don't share nursing stations,
And from birth suckle only one place.
They see effects from a sibling's libations
And hope to avoid what messed up its face!

Vervet Monkey

 is for Vervet Monkey

A male vervet monkey has features bright blue,
Which its name does not reflect.
As apparent when seen in full frontal view,
Its scrotum will not a gaze deflect.

Wildebeest

Estimates on the number of wildebeest that participate in the Greater Serengeti migration range from 1 to 1.7 million. Each year they have up to 400,000 calves almost all within a period of a few weeks. So many calves are born that even though predators may get their fill of the young wildebeest, most of them survive their attacks. The wildebeest population is limited by the supplies of grass that they encounter and devour during their yearly migration as they continually search for greener pastures. The wildebeest is also known as the gnu.

 is for Wildebeest

Serengeti plains far and near
Are oft filled with wildebeest.
When calving starts in a burst each year
It's like having flood gates released.
Though predators await upon this event
And engage in a short-lived feast,
On their prey they make not a dent
Since wildebeest multiply like yeast.

A Safari can be very Exciting.

A Lion Tree!

A Lion Beach!

 is for Exciting

Excitement awaits around the bend,
Or perhaps on the left or the right.
With hopes that the thrill will never end
A safari gives dreams day and night.

Yellow Masked Weaver

A bright yellow male masked weaver inspects the nest he has constructed to at-tract females. A female masked weaver is observing from below.

Y

is for Yellow Masked Weaver

The female masked weaver clearly found the invitation interesting!

A male masked weaver will work his tail off
Building nests to impress his dates.
To these busy birds our hats we should doff
For a fine nest turns dates into mates.

Zebra

About 200,000 to 300,000 zebras participate in the annual Serengeti migration. They specialize in eating tall grass.

Z is for Zebra

Herds of zebras migrate in vast packs,

Though they often pair up just to cover their backs.

Tall grass in the plains provides their main feast.

Short grass is then left to serve wildebeest.

The photos were all taken during a safari with Africa Dream Safaris in Tanzania between Jan 29 and Feb 7, 2016 by Huri and Stanley Fraley.

The poems are all the creation of the author with the goal of adding a touch of humor to what was an amazing experience.

The "facts" alluded to in the poems often are distorted by "poetic license" but are loosely based on real characteristics of the actual animals displayed in the photos.

Made in the USA
Charleston, SC
19 June 2016